The Ramblings of the Man Who Doesn't Want to Preach

JAMES WEBB

LIONESS
WRITING LIMITED

CONTENTS

INTRODUCTION

Browsing under the bonnet of my blog page has revealed an interesting fact. The individual post that is most frequently returned by search engines is a story I wrote in the second year of the blog. This story is clearly the one that gets the most outside exposure, and crops up on Google's search pages more often than any other.

I'd like to think that it's because the story is fantastic, but I suspect that the real reason has something to do with the fact that it's called 'The Rich Man and the Farmer'. What's happening, I reckon, is that my story is cropping up when people (or bots) search for advice on how to make lots of money, or perhaps for people who are just really interested in agriculture. I try not to think about their disappointment when they discover that my post is nothing to do with the secret of how to become fabulously wealthy, and is instead a parable about how God is actually a pretty important component of life.

But that's the point of parables isn't it? To pretend to be one thing, and then turn out to be another. To initially disappoint, but then reveal something crucially important. I'm perfectly happy if my blog posts do the same thing (I'm confident that I can deliver the disappointment part, anyway).

So here is the fourth annual collection (fourth!) of my weekly blog. I hope you're not *too* disappointed, but even if you are, I also hope that something crucially important will sneak in through the back door while you read.

The Son Who Walked

01 November 2018

The disciple sat down, cross-legged and attentive, at his master's feet.

"Teach me," he said.

"Let me tell you a story," said the master.

"There was once a man who had two sons. The eldest son was clever and handsome, while the youngest son lacked all of his brother's gifts. However, being clever and handsome does not necessarily make you a nice person. The older brother teased his younger brother mercilessly, mocking him for his lack of intellect and good looks. The younger brother didn't always understand his older brother's jokes, but he knew when he was being made fun of, and he tired of this quite quickly."

"One day the younger brother decided that he'd had enough, and that he was going to take his belongings and leave home. 'I'm going to just walk and see where my feet take me,' he said, and off he went."

3

"So, on the first day, he just walked in a straight line. But something strange began to happen. He was amazed to see that, as he passed, the animals of the forest were leaving their woodland homes to follow him."

"On the second day, he kept walking, and the trees of the forest began to uproot and join the animals following him."

"On the third day, he kept walking. As night fell, he noticed that the moon and the stars in the sky were also following him. Why was this?"

"I don't know," the disciple said.

The master smiled.

"These days, you don't need charisma or intellect. You don't even need to know where you're going. These days, if you just look like you're walking with purpose, the whole world will follow you."

World Book Day

08 November 2018

Today is World Book Day at school. Imogen is dressing up as a pirate from the *Captain Flynn* books and Xanthe is dressing up as a character from *Ratburger*. I don't know the character's name – I haven't read the book. We've planned for Parker to go as Robin Hood. He's recently enjoyed the book, and has been prepared for it for a couple of weeks. He's seemed almost excited about it at times. Granddad has repaired his bow and made him a couple of (harmless) arrows from bamboo. I bought him some camouflage trousers especially for the costume, and we've cobbled together a pretty good outfit from our dressing-up box.

I like non-school uniform days, but I don't like themed dressing-up days, for a couple of reasons. It's partly because it either costs us energy or money, neither of which we have in abundance these days, but it's mostly because we have a son with autism. He's fine with non-school uniform days, but there's something about the themed ones that set him off. Sure enough, this morning is no different.

5

Despite having plenty of advance warning and a pretty good Robin Hood costume, he's still in his pants at 8.05. He won't put anything on. What do you want to wear, Parker? "Nothing!" he says. He doesn't want to wear his costume. He doesn't want to wear non-school uniform. He doesn't want to wear school uniform. He's angry and difficult, throwing aggressive insults at everyone in the house. Normally this would cause a full-on sibling riot, but Xanthe and Imogen (to their eternal credit) have realised that this is Serious Business and are trying to help. Unfortunately, their best efforts sometimes make things worse.

"If you don't know what you want to wear, I'll choose something for you," I say. I pick out some jeans and a shirt. I dress him. He complains, but doesn't resist. I relax and go and clean-up the kitchen. I tell Imogen it's time to leave, and put her socks on for her. Xanthe has already left. Then I see a pair of jeans and a crumpled shirt at the top of the stairs. A scrawny figure in underpants runs past. I shouldn't have been surprised.

I try a different tactic. I take the underwear-clad Parker into the bathroom and we sort out his teeth and hair before going back to the bedroom. I am, unbelievably, still calm. I tell Parker that it's time to go. This has the desired effect. I have, through bitter experience, worked out that the fear of being late often steamrolls over the top of his other fears. We negotiate an outfit through trial and error ("What about this top?" "NOOO! Anything but that one!" "This one then.")

Imogen is ready, and behaving like the perfect child. Parker is now dressed, but dawdling on the issue of putting on a coat. We're finally outside, but we have to pause for a few minutes while Parker tries to break back into the house.

Then we're on our way. I am already mentally chalking this one up as a victory. Once we're underway things often calm down, and by the time we arrive at school he's usually fine. He's still angry though, and saying all kinds of nonsense to his younger sister. Every now and then she appeals to me, but mostly she ignores him. "Parker's only saying that because he's angry. He'll regret it later," she says to me, with a wisdom beyond her five years.

We get to school, but Parker hasn't calmed down.

"I really hate stupid World Book Day," he says, through tears, as we enter the school grounds.

"So do I, Parker," I reply.

My plan is to escort Parker to the door, send him in, and then walk Imogen round to her class, taking that opportunity to commend her for her stellar behaviour this morning. But Parker is in no mood to make things easy. We're at his door but he won't go in. I take him to one side, and threaten him with the loss of screen time over the weekend, but I regret it as soon as I say it. It makes things worse and he bursts into tears. It was a schoolboy error. When he's like this, threats don't work. I take it back and restore his screen privilege as only a parent can do. He calms down almost instantly, but he still won't go in.

So the three of us walk round to Imogen's door. "You've been a really good girl this morning, Imogen," I say. "Thank you." She kisses me and goes into the classroom. I take Parker back round, but he still won't go in.

"I'll walk you in," I say.

This is the Big Play, the Silver Bullet, the Nuclear Option. For Parker, there's no greater embarrassment than a parent actually being in the school building (which makes it awkward for his mum, who teaches at the school). This *always* sends him scuttling inside, but not today. It's the first time it's failed me. Instead he's physically trying to restrain me from entering the building.

"Just let me stop crying," he says. This is a fair request, so we stand to one side and I try to think of ways to cheer him up. I've got nothing.

Then Mrs Wheeler, his class's TA comes out. She's dressed as a wizard or something.

"What's wrong, Parker?" she says. Parker says nothing.

"He doesn't like World Book Day," I say.

"But you like books normally, don't you?" she says.

Parker shakes his head. A lie.

"Would you like to come and help me?" she says. "I have a few jobs I need to do before school starts."

Parker nods. Just like that, she takes him into the building, arm round his shoulders.

She's dressed as a wizard or something, but at that moment, as far as I'm concerned, she's an angel.

I know what happens next. Parker will be fine now. When I collect him later he'll be cheerful and talkative all the way home. I walk back to our house, thinking about how to reward Imogen for her maturity and grace this morning. I got Parker to school, and nothing was broken. Definitely a success, but for a weary and sensitive soul like me, successes often feel like defeats. But that's just parenting, isn't it? The rules are always changing, but you do your best, don't you?

I think I'll buy Imogen a book.

Treasure Hunt

15 November 2018

(A serious thought became this not-so-serious poem. I'm not sure that the ten-syllables per line experiment really works, nor am I totally thrilled with the final rhyme, but it'll do.)

Have you ever discovered something big

hidden away in a minuscule place?

Maybe something obvious, but more like

a raindrop that's reflecting a child's face.

We're used to seeing small things in the big,

like grains of sand hidden amongst a beach,

or the grains of truth buried deep, hidden

within a major politician's speech.

What's the biggest thing you've ever noticed

hidden away inside something that's small?

An elephant in a matchbox, perhaps,

or maybe nothing that silly at all?

As for me, I bet I've got you all beat,

for I had the most magnificent find.

You see, today I found the universe

in a scrap of bread and a sip of wine.

Look Before You Leap

22 November 2018

Travis was looking down at the piece of paper on the clipboard when he heard the polite cough. He looked up. It was Nigel.

"Hi Nigel," Travis said. "Good job today. You're demonstrating some excellent technique."

Nigel looked pleased, but only briefly. He then returned to looking like a man with something on his mind.

"Thanks Travis," he replied. "Errr, did I hear right at the end of the lesson? Something about going up in a plane next week?"

"That's right," said Travis. "We've done about as much as we can on the ground for the moment. Time to get up there, and get a taste of what it's like in the sky."

Nigel looked as though Travis had just confirmed his worst fears.

"Going up? In a plane? Why do we need to do that?"

"Like I said. Just to give you some experience," explained Travis.

"But why do we need to do that *at all*?" said Nigel.

"Sorry, mate. I'm not following."

"I'm just asking, is the plane thing compulsory?"

Travis looked confused. "Well, it is eventually, mate. You can't do skydiving without going up in a plane. The clue's in the name – *sky* diving. But don't worry. It's just a taster. No-one'll be jumping out of any planes next week."

"What?" said Nigel. "Who said anything about jumping from a plane?"

"Sorry, mate, I must be confused. You do know you've been doing skydiving lessons for the past four weeks, don't you?" said Travis.

"Yes, absolutely. That's what I signed up for."

"And that a big part of parachute jumping is the actual, you know, *jumping*."

"I signed up for skydiving lessons. I wasn't really aware that you were going to make us do an actual parachute jump at the end," said Nigel.

"Let me get this straight," said Travis carefully. "You wanted to take skydiving lessons without doing any actual skydiving?"

"That's right. You really should have made it clearer in the literature."

"Mate, I thought it was pretty clear, in the whole concept, you know? What would be the point of doing the lessons without the end product?" said Travis.

Nigel tutted, as though he'd just been told that his taxi would be five minutes late. "It's just that I don't see why I can't just have the lessons so I know what I'm doing, and leave it at that."

"Mate, it's your money, but didn't you think it a bit odd that we charged you for things like the plane and actual parachute if you weren't going to do any jumping?"

"I saw that more as a donation. To support the general concept of skydiving and subsidise those who really wanted to do the actual jumping," explained Nigel.

"And what about all the waivers we made you sign? Didn't they give you a small clue?" asked Travis.

"I signed those because I agreed with the *principles* behind them. The safety instructions and stuff. And, as I said, I'm a big supporter of the general concept of skydiving. I wouldn't have signed them if I'd known you were actually going to make *me* do it," said Nigel.

Travis shook his head. "So what's the point then? Why bother doing the lessons?"

"Well," said Nigel, beginning to get excited, "I was thinking that I could take the stuff you taught me, go home and teach my friends how to skydive. Run my own courses, as it were."

"Mate, you can't do that! It took me years to become a qualified instructor! Skydiving is dangerous!"

"Oh don't worry," said Nigel reassuringly. "None of us would actually *do* any skydiving. You wouldn't catch any of us going anywhere *near* an actual plane. No fear!"

"So you're telling me that you want to take the lessons, but not actually do the skydiving?" said Travis suspiciously.

"That's right," agreed Nigel.

"And then you want to go and teach your friends what you've learnt, and then none of you will actually do any skydiving?"

"Right again," said Nigel.

"And no-one is going to jump out of any planes?" said Travis.

"Too right," said Nigel. "Why would we want to do something like that?"

"Yeah," said Travis dryly, "what a crazy idea. Imagine learning how to do something and then actually going and doing it? Madness."

"Good, I knew you'd understand." Nigel clapped his hands together. "See you next week then…oh wait, no I won't. The week after that. No planes the week after, are there?"

"No, mate. No planes," said Travis.

"Thanks Travis," said Nigel, turning away and heading towards the exit. He called over his shoulder as he left. "Keep up the good work! You're a great teacher!"

"And you're a great pupil," Travis muttered under his breath, "but you'll never be a great skydiver."

An Advent Poem

29 November 2018

There are those who think it odd,

that you came as man and not as God.

A God would make things right

with shows of power, glory and might.

A God would shake the stage,

smiting evil-doers with holy rage.

A God, you see, will get things done.

A baby can't. He needs his mum.

A baby is no use to us;

a baby screams and makes a fuss.

A baby doesn't clear up mess,

solve problems, or bring progress.

But as for us, we're not so hot,

we're babies too, don't pretend we're not.

We need to scream, need a nappy,

we need our toys to make us happy.

We haven't grown up in years,

so only a baby could share our tears.

We're still learning how to crawl,

so I'm just thankful you came at all.

Moving Furniture

06 December 2018

When you move to a new house, you have to decide where to put the heavy furniture. The goal is to put it somewhere good, so that you won't have to move it again. If you play your cards right, you'll end up with a nice, eye-catching feature than defines the room and serves a purpose. Over the years that piece of furniture will become a comforting, familiar presence, perhaps soothing you as soon as you enter the room. Get it right, and you won't even want to move it.

But eventually it will need to be moved, and then you'll discover the delights of what lurks behind a heavy piece of furniture that has lain undisturbed for many, many months. Cobwebs and dust, yes, but also missing toys or coins, or carelessly discarded raisins and bits of dried, shriveled orange peel. There's almost no limit to the surprises waiting for you behind an immobile piece of furniture.

Now where's the heavy furniture in my soul? What are the things that I've plonked down and left untouched for years, either because they look nice where they are or because I just can't be bothered to move them? Maybe it's something that's actually impractical or even dangerous, but its constant presence has become comfortingly familiar to me. Is it time to shift something, either to get the vacuum cleaner in there, or just in case I happen to find some sparkling treasure that I thought was lost forever many years ago?

Another Advent Poem

13 December 2018

There were no lights, no holly and the ivy;

no red-breasted robin to sing in festivity;

no cheer of any sort to warm the cold winters;

no berry red Santa bringing sacks of presents,

only blood red legionaries, bringing Pax (with blades)

and the hungry hoping that it wouldn't snow.

And after all no ear did hear his coming,

because we only listen to music that we like,

and no eye did witness the raging storm

of heaven contained within tiny feet and hands,

for sometimes the first line of a poem

is best when it can only be whispered.

So into this absent-minded world of winter

(that tells itself lies to keep the dark dreams at bay),

came a mustard seed shaped Christmas,

that didn't end with an angel or a star on a tree,

and the hat that was worn for this main event

you wouldn't get from pulling any crackers.

And into this absent-minded world of winter

(that tells itself lies to keep the dark dreams at bay),

how silently, how silently,

the wondrous truth bomb is dropped,

and God imparts to human hearts

the blessings of dark dreams stopped.

The Forgotten Voice

20 December 2018

As Christmas approaches let us spend a moment remembering someone who is sometimes forgotten during this time.

No, I'm not talking about Jesus. This isn't one of those blogs.

I'm talking about someone else.

I'm talking about the early morning alarm that wakes us just before sunrise.

The dawn chorus.

The very first advent calendar.

Yes. Good old John the Baptist. He has a bit part in the nativity, remembered mostly for his prenatal acrobatics as Mary and Elizabeth share stories of motherhood, but Advent is the season of preparation for the coming of the Lord, and the first voice that called out in the wilderness, warning us of Jesus' approach, was John's.

Some of the more liturgical traditions already have us covered, clearly referencing John's role in their set readings, but others of us overlook the patron saint of Advent. God chose John to prepare the way, and every year, as we prepare anew for the coming of the Messiah, we would do well to spend a moment thinking about him.

John is the forerunner of us all. Someone like you and me, who – despite his imperfect understanding of the Son of Man and his mission – was compelled to point at Jesus and say, "Don't look at me. Instead behold the man."

Merry Christmas!

God in a Box

27 December 2018

I've been making my way through the account of Jesus' life found in Mark's Gospel recently, and through serendipity I ended up reading the Passion narrative during the week leading up to Christmas. The Resurrection arrived on Christmas day itself.

On Christmas Eve I was struck by the comparison offered by Mark 15:42-47. The season demanded that we remember the Christ being placed gently in the manger by his parents, and there I was reading about how another Joseph placed him gently in a tomb carved from rock.

Neither could hold him of course. He grew too big for the manger, and grew too alive for the tomb.

Such is the way of Jesus. He will not be 'placed' anywhere for too long. He cannot be held, trapped, nailed down, cornered, pinned, ensnared, bound, boxed in or bottled up. You may as well try and glue the sea in place. We may be more comfortable if he stays in the manger, the gentle spirit of Christmas goodwill, but he will refuse your kind offer of

27

accommodation, and wander off somewhere, life and mayhem following in his wake. Despite all the trouble he's caused me at times, he is without a doubt my favourite person ever. And despite all the trouble I've caused him, he seems quite fond of me too.

So when the Messiah who won't sit still sticks his head through your doorway and says, "I'm going out for a while. Fancy a walk?" what can you do? What can you say to that kind of invitation?

Another Year, Another Step

03 January 2019

S o how was your 2018?

A while ago I suggested that there was only one question worth asking myself in any end-of-year reflection. It's not so much about what happened, but rather how I responded. Did I grow in 2018?

As for those things that did happen, the last quarter of the year was hugely significant. We've been back from Australia for four years now, and most of that time has been spent waiting for God to make clear what kind of things I should be doing next. Every now and then I would try to take matters into my own hands, and bring order out of chaos. It didn't work. God pushed back. But since the summer, the wheels have been turning.

Since the end of August, I have started (and finished) the first draft of a novel – something I have avoided for years, because writing a book that was just one story seemed so intimidating. Since the end of August, we've moved into a new home that is much more suitable for our oversized family. Since the end of August, I have been offered a position as an 'Associate Bible Teacher' in our church, and as of January will be working part-time in this role. In other words, the days since the end of August have been constructive, focused and have given some shape to the coming months of 2019. I like shape. It agrees with me.

Seeing things fall into place has been satisfying, like placing the final piece of a particularly awkward jigsaw puzzle, but that's not the most important thing is it?

Have I grown in 2018?

I think so, yes. I've had my faith stretched in some good ways, and I've seen God work. 2018 has not left me unchanged. And that is, as always, the most important thing.

A Second Letter from God

10 January 2019

S ome of you may remember that about three years ago, Imogen wrote God a letter, the primary outcome of which seemed to be my scarring my daughter for life – or so I had thought. One day, about a year afterwards, she announced that she wanted to write to God again. It turned out that actually receiving a reply seemed to be a factor in her wanting to write a second letter. It ended up similar in content to the first one, primarily concerned with Space Hoppers it seemed. This caused me a little discouragement – I had hoped for more theological growth over the prior twelve months (When I was four years old I was already reading Calvin's 'Institutes' – *in the original French*) but you can't have everything.

Then it was my turn to freak out a little. What had I started? Now I would have to write a reply, like last time. I wasn't sure where to go with it. Imogen is our fifth child, and pretty much the only one I think I haven't managed to break so far, but if I went around pretending to be God all the time then her odds weren't great. In the end I sat down and thought, "What do I think God would want to say to Imogen at this moment?" and it all came quite easily after that.

It doesn't matter how clever we are, or aren't. How eloquent and well-read. How persuasive. None of that matters, not really. We will never be more influential or powerful in our words than when we are doing nothing more than giving a voice to what the Holy Spirit is already whispering to somebody's heart.

"What should I say?" is a decent question.

"What do I think God would want to say to this person at this moment?" is a better one.

The Best Room in the World

17 January 2019

The other day I was walking aimlessly around the church building, and I found myself wandering down a corridor I had never been down before. I'm not usually the adventurous type, but I thought I'd see where it ended up. At the end of the corridor was a big, thick, old wooden door. As I said, I'm not the adventurous type, but I took a look anyway.

The door opened into a large room, and it was absolutely *full* of people. There were all kinds in there, old and young, men and women. Anyone that you could imagine was there, and they were all busy with something. There was a group of people painting the walls, and a group of people setting out chairs, and a group of people cleaning the carpets, and all sorts of things going on.

I thought they must be preparing for some type of church service or something. Everyone was working so hard, and the room looked *amazing*. I mean, it's hard to get the feel of a room right sometimes, but these people had nailed it. The way that everything was set out, the colours of the walls and carpet, the clean windows, the smell. I don't know exactly what it was, but it was without a doubt, hands-down, the best room I had ever seen anywhere in any church ever.

I stood in the doorway watching them work for a while. One of the painters ended up near me, meticulously applying some magnolia to the wall beside to the door.

"What time does it start?" I said.

"What?" he said without looking at me. He was giving all of his concentration to the painting.

"The service, or whatever it is you have here. What time does it start?"

"I don't know," he said.

"It must be soon though? The way everyone's working so hard."

"I don't know," he said.

"Well, how long have you been doing this?" I said.

He stopped painting long enough to shrug. "A while. Days. Months. Maybe longer."

"Months?" I looked around the room. All these people working so hard. For months? "But it shouldn't take months to get a room ready, should it?"

"The wall could always do with another coat," he said. "You know how it is. You've just finished and then you notice a patch that needs touching up. A fingerprint or smear that needs covering. It's the same with the carpet. And you'd be surprised at how much work has to go into getting the chairs *just right*."

"But why?" I said.

"What do you mean?" he said.

"Why are you doing this?"

He finally turned his attention to me. "Because the room has to be ready. We have to work hard to get the room ready. It's the way to please God."

"Really?" I said.

"Yeah," the man said. "God wants us to work hard. It pleases Him. Then we get to go and be with Him forever."

"Huh," I said. "I didn't know that."

"That's how it is. Would you like to join us? The guys in the kitchen could always do with one more. There's just so much washing up."

"No, you're alright," I said. I looked at the watch I wasn't wearing. "I think I'll be going now."

"It's your soul," said the man. He went back to his painting.

I backed out of the room and carefully shut the door. As I turned to leave, I saw the sign above the door. It was quite small. I hadn't noticed it before. It read 'Welcome to Hell'.

Fearless

24 January 2018

(Our church's annual Week of Prayer (we do pray at other times too) rolled around again, and once more I was asked to write one of the devotional reflections for the week. I'm posting it as this week's blog post, just because I can.)

L et's start these devotions for the Week of Prayer in an unconventional way – with some words from the 14th century Persian poet, Hafiz:

Fear is the cheapest room in the house

I would like to see you living

In better conditions.

I don't know about you, but I can imagine God saying these exact words to each and every one of us. In fact, He does say these words, or words like them, through Paul in Romans 8:14:

"For you did not receive a spirit that makes you a slave again to fear, but you received the spirit of sonship."

Fear is the cheapest room in the house, and God would like to see us living in better conditions.

Fear is a powerful thing. Fear makes us work hard. From a distance, frightened people look motivated, conscientious and diligent. But God would like to see us living in better conditions.

Too many of us let our lives be controlled by fear. Fear of failure, fear of poverty, fear of criticism, fear of embarrassment, fear of conflict. So many different fears. But God would like to see us living in better conditions.

As we head into this week, know that prayer is one of the gifts given by God to help keep fear out of our hearts; to help us take those first steps towards fearless living. It says as much in Philippians 4:6 & 7:

"Do not be anxious about anything, but in every situation, by prayer and petition, with thanksgiving, present your requests to God. And the peace of God, which transcends all understanding, will guard your hearts and minds in Christ Jesus."

Perhaps this week will finally be the time for you to make the move into some more suitable accommodation?

Imagine That

31 January 2019

I have an overactive imagination. Sometimes it's good, sometimes it isn't. It's helpful for my writing, for one thing, but on the other hand, it's very easy for me to miss what God is doing right in front of my face because I've drifted off into one daydream or another.

I grew up with the conviction that a lively imagination wasn't a particularly 'Christian' trait. Certainly, some branches of our faith have an extreme suspicion of anything fantastical or abstract. I once asked my friend Terry why he thought some Christians had such a problem with imaginary worlds, and he wondered whether it was because heresy begins in the imagination, and therefore the imagination is considered a dangerous place not to be trusted – a kind of spiritual Wild West. I think he might have been on to something.

Anyway, I've finally come to realise that imagination, like most things, is actually one of the parts of Himself that God gives to us. He blesses some of us with a mind like a razor blade, able to hold focus and slice through nonsense with surgical precision. He gives others of us a mind like a sponge, that soaks up the colour and music of the world, and mixes them together into some new work of art. Both of these minds come from God, and both of them need to be submitted to Him before we can use them well.

Imagination is the ability to envision a different world. Can the Kingdom of God ever come before someone first says, "I wonder what life would be like if…"? Back in Genesis, before God actually performs the act of cobbling together a human being, He first says, "Let us make something different now. Something more like us than anything else we've made so far." In short, God *imagined* us before He made us. For God, the two might even be the same thing. The ability to create new worlds in the mind is not from the enemy, but from the Father. The trick is to create the kind of world that He looks at and says, "Hey, that's a good effort!"

Using your imagination is a spiritual discipline, and one that I think God would like us to enjoy on a regular basis. If you're not convinced then go off and read Ephesians 3:20. To me, that sound like God's laying down a challenge…

The Jeremiah Blues

07 February 2019

So God says "Go!" and you say, "No, I've worn

These shoes before. I know the way this ends.

With me abused, misused, confused and bruised,

I wonder why you don't have any friends?"

Still God says "Go!" and you say, "So, no peace

Allowed, it seems. It's gone from bad to worse.

Inside my chest I've wrath yet to express,

But tell me why your blessing is a curse?"

So you say, "Fine," and God says, "Wait! Let's get

This straight. A little prophet can't compete.

You forget, dead set, I'm not in your debt.

Don't race me, I'm a rocket – you're just feet.

"Now listen, there's a vacancy to fill:

Tester of Metals. I'll be very frank.

Best of the rest, your C.V. has impressed,

But partly because it was mostly blank.

"My words disturb the peace and when it comes

To choosing mouths I've impeccable taste.

The LORD of night and song, of right and wrong

And I don't need to rhyme to make my point.

"So hold your nerve, that's what a prophet does.

Refine and test. You'll teach them how to wail.

No balm in Gilead – be mad not sad,

Flame like a holy Molotov cocktail.

"Each prophet needs a message to proclaim;

A god to follow; fire to throw themselves

Upon. Be strong. Let baby Babylon

Go. Speak! The sleepless inner pyre compels!

"I understand. It's struggle to be called.

Do your best. Stand up tall. We'll muddle through.

Confused, abused and bruised, but not misused.

So go! We've work still to do, me and you."

Saying "Yes" and Doing What You're Told

14 February 2019

As you might have been able to tell from last week's post, I'm making my way through Jeremiah again. I've always had a soft spot for this particular jolly prophet. I think his melancholy, dragging-his-heels approach to obedience struck a chord with me long ago, and over the years my appreciation for his own brand of bickering faithfulness has only grown. There are two specific things that I think Jeremiah grokked that are worth careful consideration:

First, saying "Yes" to God is serious business. It's not like changing your energy supplier. It's a solemn and sinister thing, and you can't take those words back. Jeremiah knew that a "Yes" to God meant a "No" to a quiet life. I wonder how many of us sign up without reading the small print? Jeremiah was, at least, under no illusions about what obedience meant. There's a wise honesty in his moaning reluctance.

Second, sometimes you just have to do what you're told. That's a part of the Christian walk that is hard to make sound appealing or reasonable, but that's just the way it is. There are no short cuts, no letters from a parent excusing you from P.E. here. Sometimes God just says, "Get on with it," and ignores your whining "Why?". In Jeremiah's case, when he tried to blackmail God with his silence, the Holy Spirit just built up and up until the prophet thought that he would explode. This was a kindness on God's part – honestly, if there's something you know you have to do but don't want to, you could try asking God to not let you have any rest until you've done it. But if you do, don't blame me for the sleepless nights and fire in your bones. It's all on you.

Does this post sounds a little heavy? Maybe it's because I'm reading Jeremiah. But I'm reading it with a smile on my lips, because I know that it's the story of a man who has a deep and robust relationship with God. A man who feels close enough to God to moan and complain, but then to pick himself up, dust himself down and get on with the task at hand anyway. That's the sort of man I'd like to be.

The Sacrament of Having Your Earwax Removed

21 February 2019

As I write this, my right ear is totally blocked with wax.

Apparently, according to my doctor, I either have very small or very dry ear canals. Whatever.

These days they don't just syringe the ear to dislodge the offending build-up. No. Now you have to wait two weeks to get a jet of water pumped into your ear. In those two weeks you're supposed to, twice a day, lie on your side with an ear full of olive oil to soften up the wax in preparation for the actual event.

Because I'm me, I can't stop myself from reaching the conclusion that having wax removed in this manner is actually sacramental.

Hear me out (pun intended).

One of the common definitions of a sacrament is a 'visible sign of an invisible grace'. At the moment, my ear is blocked. The act of having an ear cleansed removes the blockage; opens up the pathway.; *literally* opens one's ear to hear. Is this not a visible sign of the invisible grace that the Holy Spirit bestows upon us? Just as baptism is an image of the spiritual act of death and resurrection, having wax removed is an image of the renewing action of the Holy Spirit.

Plus, the procedure involves oil and water, two of the most sacramental aspects of creation.

Amen?

Amen!

OK, I'm only (partly) joking, but it does remind me of a more serious thought.

Namely, if you know *how* to look, you can find God everywhere in the day-to-day.

A Balanced Diet

28 February 2019

A while ago I had an idea for a short story that went under the name 'A Balanced Diet'. It was about a boy who has a revelation whilst listening to a talk at the church that his family attends. The talk, aimed at children, was on the book of Job, and the revelation is this: If you're really naughty then God'll get you, but if you're really good then the devil gets you, as Job experienced. The boy decides that the best thing to do is to be neither good nor bad, but to try and fly under the radar by living a balanced diet, so to speak. Whenever he does anything bad, he immediately has to find something good to do in order to balance it out, so as to not attract any unwanted supernatural attention. Of course, the opposite is true as well. If his mother praises him for doing a good job of tidying his room, he has to balance that out by sneaking off and pinching his baby brother or something.

I didn't get far with it – just an idea and the beginnings of a tale – but I know, even without exploring it, that it will end up in a dark place. That's where selfishness, fear and manipulation always end up. A dark place.

The alternative, and the only route to the light, is surrender. I've been coming to realise that. Note that surrender is not the same as 'giving up' or 'not caring' or 'abdicating responsibility'. Surrender is the act of trying, caring and taking responsibility, but only for and about those things that God has given you to try, care and take responsibility for. In other words, what you are surrendering is your demand to set the agenda.

The story I haven't written is about a boy who is trying to set the agenda. If I do ever sit down to write it, it will end up in a dark place. Submit to God, let Him set the agenda, and though you may at times find yourself wandering through some dark places you'll never end there. You'll just be passing through on your way to the light.

Ash Friday

7 March 2019

What can you build from dust and ashes?

From remnants scattered after flames?

Wealth of a life all burnt, destroyed,

Nothing of joy or hope remains.

What can you build from dust and ashes?

From sons of sacrifice and strife?

Stretched on a cross, the Man of Sorrows,

They tell me He can build a life.

The First Vision of an Unwelcome Jesus

14 March 2018

There you are, just sitting, living your life and minding your own business, when there's a knock at the door.

You get up and answer it.

It's Jesus. He's got a parcel for you.

"What is it?" you say.

"Forgiveness of sins," he says. "Eternal life. My presence with you every day. And more."

"Cool," you say.

He places the parcel on the ground, and offers you a yellow document.

"Read this, and sign here," he says, indicating the line at the bottom of the page. He hands you a pen.

You glance at the document. Everything seems to be in order. You can't wait to get your hands on that parcel. You sign.

***

Some time passes. Years maybe. There's a knock at the door.

You get up to answer it, but you don't get the chance. The door swings open before you can get there.

It's Jesus.

"I've got something for you to do," he says. "Grab your stuff and let's go – no, in fact, don't grab your stuff. There isn't time. Let's just go now. Follow me."

And you say, "What?"

Jesus fixes you with a stare, and then waves a yellow document in your face.

"Is this your signature?" he says.

And you say, "Ah."

"Did you read the document before you signed it? Did you read it all?" he says.

And you say, "Ah."

"You didn't read it? I told you to read it. Count the cost. Don't start a fight without knowing whether or not you can go the distance – I said that. Did you not read it?"

And you say, "Ah."

The Second Vision of an Unwelcome Jesus

21 March 2018

One Saturday, many years ago, Ruth and I were travelling to London by train. We were sitting, waiting for the train to depart, when a couple and their young daughter got on. The man found a seat, but the woman stood by the open door, finishing her cigarette. The young girl, who must have been maybe five or six years old, began to speak

"Mum," she said, "Mum. You're not allowed to smoke on the train."

Mum ignored Daughter and carried on smoking.

Daughter tried again. "Mum, you're not allowed to smoke on the train. You'll get told off."

"I don't care," said Mum.

That got to me. I could make allowances for Mum, finishing off her cigarette by the open door before the train departed, but "I don't care"? Those three little words infuriated me. She didn't care. She didn't care what her daughter was saying. She probably didn't care about anyone else but herself. I was seething.

Inwardly.

I didn't say anything. Of course I didn't. I'm British.

Daughter kept going, bless her little cotton socks. "Mum! Mum!"

I didn't say anything. At least, not out loud.

But in my mind's eye, I was very vocal. I pictured myself saying something scathing to Mum. Something like, "Excuse me, why don't you listen to your daughter? She obviously has more brains than you do."

These days, I believe they call that a 'sick burn'.

In my mind's eye, Mum was embarrassed by my biting remark, and slunk away in humiliation. I was bathed in a smug glow. I sure showed her! She won't smoke by an open door again in a hurry!

In my mind's eye.

But in my mind's eye, I saw someone else. Sitting on a chair opposite me. A man. Early thirties. He looked like a manual worker, a carpenter or something, from somewhere in the Middle East. Maybe a place called Galilee.

He looked troubled. He was rubbing his wrists and hands.

"Are you OK?" I asked – in my mind's eye.

"I'm OK," he replied. "It's just these old wounds I have. They give me trouble sometimes."

As I sat back, and the journey began, I knew right away what was causing his injuries to flare up.

And it wasn't Mum.

The Overachiever

28 March 2019

For many years I've been haunted by the spectre of underachievement. I've been convinced that I should have got more done by now; made more of a difference; that I've fallen well short of my potential. I've spent large chunks of my life frustrated with myself. It's a form of perfectionism that has, at times, both motivated me and made me miserable.

Way back in time, when I was a student in London, I was prayed for by someone who gave me a reference from the Bible – 2 Corinthians 12:7-10. For those of you who don't know, this is the passage where Paul talks about his 'thorn in the flesh' and how difficult it has made his life. Paul goes on to explain that God didn't answer his prayer to take this problem away because it kept him grounded in the grace of God and prevented his own personal strength from getting in God's way. The person who prayed for me made no suggestions as to why they felt that this reference was significant, but I've always had it in the back of my mind. In fact, it was the start of a journey that led to me eventually writing my Master's dissertation on the subject of suffering, though over the years I couldn't really see how it linked directly to my life.

One of the benefits of getting older, at least in the way that I have gotten older, is that you begin to understand yourself better. I know that I am highly sensitive (i.e. often too sensitive); that I struggle with stress and high pressure situations; that I am introverted to an above-average level; that I don't adapt well to change and so on. Yet, somehow, I find myself living a life that works against all those things. At some point you have to ask yourself what's going on.

The truth is, I know full well what my life would have looked like if it weren't for God. I would have found an easy, low-stress job, and settled down until retirement. I definitely wouldn't have five children. I would spend every evening and weekend playing video games and eating fast food. I know that's what I would have been because, even as I write, there's a part of me that cannot deny how appealing such a life sounds. But, alas, it wasn't to be.

At some point in the past twelve months, I can't be sure exactly when, it all began to make sense. My personality, the things that make it so hard for me to do what I feel God has wanted me to do, is my thorn. That's the thing that has threatened to cripple me, and left me saying – so many times over the years – "God, why did you make me this way if you wanted me to do all these crazy things that you keep asking me to do? Surely you could have picked someone better equipped for this?" The thorn in my flesh is me, it's who I am. It's a weakness that constantly seeks to undermine everything I do. I wish I was a different, more dynamic, more robust person, but I am not.

But I also have finally understood the significance of the verses in 2 Corinthians. What was true for Paul is true for me too. A man like me should either be a terminally lazy couch-potato, or have been irredeemably shattered by the cavalcade of stressful situations and ridiculous requests that life has dumped on him. But I am neither of those things, because the words that God spilled onto Paul are also meant for me: *"My grace is sufficient for you, for my power is made perfect in weakness."*

I am an atheist's worst nightmare, because a man like me shouldn't exist. My life only makes sense if God is true, and as such – just like Paul – the glory becomes His. The house that He has somehow managed to build on such fragile foundations testifies to His skill as an architect, not to my greatness.

And it means that the spectre of underachievement can finally be laid to rest. I am actually an overachiever. I *shouldn't* have managed to do half the things that I have done. Every sermon; every page written; every line of poetry is an over-achievement, and what's insane is that I suspect that God's not finished with me yet.

"But as for me, I shall always have hope;

I will praise you more and more."

Psalm 71:14

Halfway There

04 April 2019

We're about halfway through Lent – the length of time where we prepare for the good news that Jesus would not stay dead.

I think I like the idea of Lent more than I like Lent itself. Don't get me wrong, I think Lent is a good thing – a timely and excellent reminder – and I'm sure that many people benefit from its place in the calendar. However, because things like reflection, discipline and ritual all have an important home in my spirituality, I don't think that they're tools that should just be dragged out of storage for a forty-day chunk of the year. I try to make them a regular habit and so that aspect of Lent seems – dare I say it – a tad redundant to me.

Furthermore, Easter is not a time where things slow down and opportunities for reflection increase – quite the opposite. I imagine many of you face the same situation. For me, Easter sees an increase in workload regarding children, family, school and church. Making time for solitude and space for reflection feels like even more of a luxury at this time of the year, so I'm grateful that it's already a part of my life. Instead my greatest need during the March/April madness is to make sure that I'm constantly inviting God into the middle of whatever smoke and thunder makes up my life each day.

Although it's important and totally right to celebrate Easter each year, I know that I need Jesus and his resurrection every day of my life. I suppose that my hope is that I carry the attitudes of Lent with me 365 days a year, instead of for just forty.

A Different Perspective

11 April 2019

I'm making a conscious effort in 2019 to develop my skill at writing poetry. I'm trying to learn and understand the rules, with marginal success, though you may notice an increase in the amount of poetry that appears on the blog as I experiment. You are nothing more than guinea pigs to me.

Anyway, I was reading a poem that referenced the story in Mark 2, where Jesus heals the paralytic man who is lowered through the roof by his friends, and it gave me a crazy idea – how about writing a different poem for every story in Mark's gospel? It's an ambitious project that I have no intention of actually *starting* any time soon, but it'll sit there on the back burner of my mind for the coming years. Never say never.

The thing about setting the gospel stories to poetry is that it encourages you to come at them from an uncommon angle. It's not too different to the way I like to construct a sermon in that regard. For example, take the story in Mark 2. It's familiar to many of us, with familiar points and familiar conclusions, but I was thinking about it from a different perspective this morning.

I imagined myself sitting there, in my small, enclosed room, with Jesus, listening to him teaching and speaking. That's where I want to be. I'm perfectly happy there. But there's a world of hurt outside; a world that I'm actually supposed to be engaging with and bringing healing to. Sometimes I forget that world's there, and I lose myself in blissful isolation that has warped from something important into something selfish. As much as it annoys me to be covered in falling plaster, I sometimes need the hurting world to intrude and forcefully interrupt my naval-gazing. It reminds me that there are people outside, and by making a great hole in the roof they are letting fresh air into my world and giving me a glimpse of the sky.

If I ever get round to writing a poem on Mark 2, that's what it will be about.

Bank Holiday

18 April 2019

(I warned you that I'd be writing more poetry. Good poetry doesn't need an explanation, so you can be sure that what follows is not a good poem. It came out of a thought I'm sure many of you have had; Easter is now so normalised that it can be easy – even for followers of Jesus – to take for granted things that shouldn't be. Anyway, it's not a great poem, and comes across a bit more cynical than I'd like. I don't want you to think that I'm some kind of Easter Scrooge – I actually quite like chocolate eggs and holidays, but I also quite like the last two lines. If I had the time I'd try and fix what I think is wrong with it, but there's an Easter blog due, so…)

The sun shone on the day love died

As though nothing was wrong.

The world smiled on the day love died.

They didn't know, they carried on.

Crime was done on the day love died

And resisting arrest.

Washing was done on the day love died,

Dried and folded and pressed.

So life went on the day love died,

No-one batted an eye.

Who had noticed that love had died?

Who had said a good-bye?

Love died, take a day off to raise some hell.

Love rose, so let's have Monday off as well.

This Post-Easter Blog is Far Too Long

25 April 2019

Sometimes a song or a story or a poem will generate a powerful emotional response in me by putting into words something that is buried deep within, something I haven't really given shape to myself yet. This is what art does. Why, just the other day I was listening to someone explain how he had been left shaken by listening to a short story that somehow managed to encapsulate his own experience of childhood.

The thing is, I'm beginning to wonder if this is enough. I suspect that this moment of connection, powerful as it is, is only half the job. Can't art move beyond just identifying with our problems, to actually providing a solution? Surely it can go beyond just dredging up pain. Can't art also offer healing?

I suppose that naming the problem is the first step to healing, but I can't help but feel that many people are content to be stirred up, and never take those next steps towards wholeness.

As we collectively march down the highway of individualism (irony intended), I get the impression that we lionise this idea of identification. In short, it's enough to form groups of like-minded, like-souled people who share our hurts. We don't necessarily want to get better. We don't want to change. We want to be around people who cry with us, nod and say, "Me too!" We think that's enough. We think that sharing war stories is as good as community gets.

I've pondered this obsession with 'being understood' for a while now. In *The Second Listening Book* I wrote a silly thing called 'Narrow Road' which was about this very subject – how we seek advice from people who have made our mistakes rather than from people who had the wisdom to avoid making our mistakes.

The ultimate destination of this thinking for the Christian is that the Cross primarily becomes the place where God identifies with human suffering, rather than the place where God deals with sin and provides the conclusion to the drama of our condition. It's absolutely true and beautiful that, in Christ, God shares our sufferings, but that would never be enough for God and we should never settle for that ourselves. God's agenda is not for us to be understood but for us to be healed.

George Herbert's poem 'Easter' includes the following stanza:

Awake, my lute, and struggle for thy part
With all thy art.
The crosse taught all wood to resound his name,
Who bore the same.
His stretched sinews taught all strings, what key
Is best to celebrate this most high day.

I think it was a stroke of genius, by old George here, to paint an image of the Cross as the inspiration for all musical instruments offered up in worship. And it has always captivated me, this idea that the Cross is the foundation of truly powerful works of art. It makes sense. The Cross is the place where our hurts are unearthed and brought to the surface, but only so that we can be made whole again. I would like art to strive for the same goal: not just the stirring of the soul, but the healing of it.

Communion of the Saints

02 May 2019

The twelfth chapter of Hebrews starts with a vaguely threatening verse: 'Therefore, since we are surrounded by such a great cloud of witnesses, let us throw off everything that so easily entangles, and let us run with perseverance the race marked out for us.'

I used to think that the writer of the letter was basically saying, "Look, you're being watched *all the time*, so there's your incentive to not mess it up." It wasn't a particularly encouraging thought, to imagine this great cloud of eyebrows being raised in collective disappointment whenever I put a foot wrong. Of course, a few theology degrees later, I have realised that this is not what the author of Hebrews meant. The great cloud of witnesses being referred to is the list of heroes of the faith from the previous chapter; those who have gone before us. They were witnesses in that their lives testified to God being at work. The writer of the letter is actually saying, "Be encouraged by all the fine men and women who have gone before you. Let their example spur you on to greatness."

That's a much more effective encouragement, and far less creepy in an "*I see dead people*" way.

One of the statements of the Apostle's Creed is 'We believe in the communion of the saints'. There's probably a few Protestants who are not quite sure what they're agreeing to when they say this. It all sounds suspiciously Catholic. Of course, it's one of those statements that allows you to put your own particular denominational spin on it, but I interpret it in a Hebrews 12:1 way. I am in communion with all followers of God, past and present, not because they remain around like Force ghosts from *Star Wars*, but rather because I follow in their footsteps, learn from them and know that they stand alongside me. For example, I have never met Richard Wurmbrand but his writings have had such an influence on me that I feel like I have been discipled by him. He is just one of many of the saints, living and dead, who have strengthened my story through their words and their example – just like in Hebrews 11 & 12.

Any attempt to genuinely live a life with God at the centre can easily make you feel like you are in a minority, but being in a minority is not the same as being alone. I believe, and will always believe, in the communion of the saints.

Choking on the Hand that Feeds Me

09 May 2019

Remember being at school, when popularity was such a big part of life? That was the top of the food chain back then – being popular; being one of the 'cool kids'. Then we left school and marched off into adult life, but it seems that the playground followed us.

Who's that person telling me what I want to hear, giving me what I want? Is it a politician or is it a contestant on *Britain's Got Talent*? I don't think I can tell the difference these days. Either way, all they want is to get my support; all they want is to be popular.

We've got this thing called Fake News now, telling you what you already want to believe. It spreads, and as it becomes popular, it also becomes true, like some horrible alien that first infects and then replaces its host. You've seen *The Thing*, right?

And then there's the internet, which just goes to show that even though we're older, we haven't really grown up. How many friends, votes, likes, subscribers? What are the best sites on the Internet? The most popular ones. Why are they popular?

Because they're the best. Everyone still wants to copy the cool kids.

This is the human condition – a tireless search for meaning and acceptance, and the delusion that popularity means both. When there is no God, we can only feed off each other.

Do Christians run on the same fuel? Do churches, preachers, websites, and books chase popularity as though it were some proof of authenticity? Is that what it's all about in the end? Being popular? Being liked? Being acceptable? Is giving people what they want the same as giving people the Kingdom of God?

Jesus' heart was broken once: "I have come to bring fire on the earth, and how I wish it were already kindled!"

My dear Lord Jesus. I'm afraid that were you to come to us today you might struggle to find even twelve…

Rewriting the Story

16 May 2019

For years I had been labouring under the illusion that I should write short stories, because they were less work than writing novels. I can tell you now that it doesn't matter how long your story is, a short attention span is a bad thing regardless. Something changed for me last summer, when motivation aligned with idea and I spent the last months of 2018 hammering away at my keyboard, trying to churn out at least one thousand words a day for my magnum opus, the book that they would plant at my grave instead of a headstone. By the end of November I had finished my first draft, just over 120,000 words that were all arranged in an order that told a story. Then I did what any writer worth his or her salt will tell you to do – I walked away from it for a while.

I went back a little later and went through it. It turned out that it was mostly 120,000 very bad words, but buried in those very bad words was A Decent Story. That was satisfying for me, especially as A Decent Story hadn't been in there from the start. At the beginning it was just a faint idea in a skeleton world, but the process of writing firmed up the idea and put flesh on the bones of the world. And Lo, James Saw That It Was Decent.

So a few more months later, I've started the second draft. I wasn't quite sure what a second draft would look like, but I can tell you now that my second draft is actually an entire rewrite. I might be able to salvage a few likeable paragraphs from the first draft, but I'm starting from scratch and doing the whole thing again, and I'm finding it energising rather than demoralising. You see, the first draft was me figuring out the story. Huge parts of the world changed as I wrote; major characters invited themselves into the story halfway through; I didn't really know my heroes when I was writing those early chapters of the first draft. This second draft allows me to go back and start from the beginning, knowing what I now know about the end. I can introduce those major characters from the start of the story, have my heroes make a consistent journey, and foreshadow the richness of the setting from page one. In short, I can tell a better story now that I know where it's supposed to end up.

Lots of writers would argue that it's better to let your characters arrive at the ending without your help, and suggest I might be breaking that cardinal rule by already having a concrete destination. I see their point, and completely agree that a writer should always try to let the characters make the decisions and say the words, but I'm not ashamed of the fact that I have a vision for the world I've made. After all, I'm created in the image of the storyteller God and He's always known how it's supposed to end. The first draft was a journey for myself and for my characters, and the second draft will be the same, but this time I know them, and I know the world that they live in, and the story is always better when it's told by one who knows.

Ironical Preaching

23 May 2019

I preached a sermon this week; the main thrust of which was the message that God does not demand perfection of us. Afterwards, I sat down, feeling flat and disappointed because I felt like the sermon hadn't gone perfectly.

I must be growing, because it only took me a few moments to realise the irony of the situation.

Anyway, it made me think about other ironic post-sermon moments. Here's a short list that I came up with. They are, of course, all fictional. Any resemblance to actual persons, living or dead, or actual events is purely coincidental etc. etc. I deny everything.

Preaching a sermon on how we need to get our approval from God, and then hanging around at the back of the church looking pitiful so that someone will come up to you and tell you that your sermon was good.

Preaching a sermon about bearing patiently with one another, and then picturing what it would be like to slowly roast over an open fire the particular member of the congregation who has come up to you to pick holes in your talk.

Preaching a sermon on the centrality of worship, and then spending the closing songs thinking about how glad you are that the sermon is over, and wondering what you're going to spend the afternoon doing.

Preaching a sermon on the need to have the courage of your convictions, and then sneaking out of church before anyone can ask you any difficult faith-related questions.

Preaching a sermon on humility, and then not listening to the closing prayer because you're too busy reflecting on how well the sermon went and what an exceptionally brilliant preacher you've turned out to be.

Preaching a sermon on being honest with other people and God, and then telling anyone who asks that your week has been 'fine'.

See, it's easy. I bet you could come up with a few of your own. Feel free to post them in the comments if you do.

Ascension Day

30 May 2019

Today is Ascension Day, a religious festival that seems to sneak past most of us every year. It marks the ascension of Christ into heaven, as detailed in Acts 1. I feel like it deserves a bit more recognition than it gets. It's a significant moment.

The ascension of Jesus marks the start of something quite spectacular. He leaves so that the Comforter can be sent. Ascension Day bleeds into Pentecost; you cannot have one without the other, and it's with good reason that we make a big deal about Pentecost (or at least we should). This is not just Jesus moving on, as though he were catching a flight home after his summer holiday. This is setting up for a seismic spiritual shift. The ball starts rolling towards that time when God will be present, in power, with each and every believer at all times. I don't think Satan likes Ascension Day one single bit.

But that's not all. The relevant line in the Apostle's Creed is 'He ascended into heaven, and is seated at the right hand of the Father'. At first this may seem like the answer to a question that nobody asked: Where is Jesus now? But even this is glorious. The New Testament repeatedly drip feeds us this idea that Christ is now at God's right hand (Acts 7:55-56, Romans 8:34, Ephesians 1:20 and others). What's the significance of this? Well, apart from the connotations that this is a place of power and authority, there is something else I want to remind you of today.

You can find it in the Romans verse mentioned above. Paul doesn't just tell us where Jesus is, but what he's doing: Christ is at the right hand of the Father interceding for us, his brothers and sisters, while we go about our business. What are God and Jesus talking about at this moment? Us. You.

When I think about this, I think of another moment in God's Story. Jesus is talking to Peter, breaking the bad news to him that Satan is going to kick him while he's down, and that his immediate future involves failure. And then in Luke 22:32 Jesus drops this line: "But I have prayed for you, Simon, that your faith may not fail. And when you have turned back, strengthen your brothers and sisters."

Jesus prayed for Simon Peter, and look what he did with his restored life. Even if our own lives are pockmarked with failure, redemption and restoration are always an option, because Jesus is at the right hand of the Father interceding for each of us.

And, just think, you wouldn't get any of this without Ascension Day.

Intercession

06 June 2019

(I'm having one of my 'stretched' times at the moment, and writing a fresh and engaging blog post seems like a bridge too far. The good news is that's been a while since I inflicted one of my experiments in poetry on you, so here's one that I've had sitting around for just a moment like this. I'm not going to apologise…)

braham,

Pushing Him in the chest,

Tries

To hold His breath.

King Canute of the Covenant.

Could there be tears

There

On His face? Not just wrath,

As it burns?

Shame on Him?

No, shame on us. For He

Tries

Integrity.

"Who will stand in the breach for them?"

He asks of us.

There

We sit in the rubble

And throw stones.

The Inconvenience of Forgiveness

13 June 2019

I've just written a blog post.

But not this blog post.

I was reflecting on something that had happened to me years ago, and I thought the experience would make a good post. It was an interesting situation, personal and significant, with a strong applicable lesson at the end. In short, it was perfect blog material.

So I wrote it. It was pretty good.

But…

It was a story about how someone had let me down. The blog didn't mention any names, but it had some specific details. It needed to, for the story to work. It had happened a long time ago, but anyone who knew my history might have been able to work out exactly who the villain of the piece was.

(Don't worry. It wasn't you. Probably.)

And that was a problem.

Because if I've forgiven, then I've made a decision to carry the cost of another's sin. That means not dragging their name through the mud. It means protecting their dignity where possible. It means not naming and shaming.

So, I sat there with a perfectly good blog post (and those are an increasingly rare commodity, let me tell you) and I knew that if I really had forgiven, I couldn't use it.

So I deleted it.

And wrote this instead.

A Fifth of a Century

20 June 2019

I don't have much to say this week, which is fine. I've been talking a lot recently.

All I want to announce is that, as of yesterday, Ruth and I have been married for twenty years.

I know that doesn't sound like much to some of you, but it's kind of a big deal to me. Not because I'm amazed that we've lasted this long, or anything like that. Rather, because it's an opportunity for me to reflect, and in doing so confirm something that I've known for a while – namely that I'm happier with my marriage now than I was when we first started out two decades ago.

I know, just from life, that being happily married is not something to take for granted; despite what certain movies might imply, it doesn't just happen. Ruth and I have worked at it over the years, and it's paid off in spades. I can't think of any twenty year project that would have been as rewarding as my marriage.

That is, in part, because I am still in love with my wife. And that is, in part, because over the past twenty years she has just become more lovable.

Anyway, thank you Ruth, and thank you for reading this far.

Normal service will be resumed next week.

A Typical Morning

27 June 2019

Reid has already left for school with his mum, while Calvin sleeps on in his GCSE-free zone. Xanthe is somewhere in the house, killing time by listening to music at a volume chosen for the purpose of agitating her younger brother. I ask Parker about his homework. He declares in a loud voice that he needs some alone time and marches out into the garden. Imogen, sitting at the table munching on her cereal, doesn't even look up from her book.

A typical morning.

I return to the sink, where I am halfway through some washing up. There are lots of bubbles. It's the bubbles that make things clean, after all. They form a sheet over the water, and ripple as I disturb them. The bubbles are connected to one another in a crazy patchwork, but they burst and break if pushed too far. A bit like a family, I suppose. Is God in the bubbles?

My mind is full of what's-on-today thoughts, trying to arrange everything like a sliding puzzle with more pieces than spaces. I am weary, and not much looking forward to what is to come.

A typical morning.

I wash up a few items – those not worthy of the dishwasher. I try and identify those moments of time in the day when I can squeeze in a little more activity; some unscheduled task. It's what I normally do, which is to try and front-load the beginning of the week, so that I can take a bit of a breather as the weekend approaches. I'm not sure how efficient or healthy it is, but it's how I operate.

Things get washed up. I begin tidying up the mess that is caused by washing up. What a world, where cleaning stuff makes other stuff dirty. Parker comes inside, having had his 'alone time', and talks to me briefly about his homework. Imogen has finished her breakfast and disappeared. Xanthe's music has gone quiet- she has relocated somewhere else in the final few minutes before she is due to leave. Calvin will not be seen for at least another hour.

The sun is somewhere out there, behind the summer clouds. The sun is always there, buried, and even weariness and dread will not quench it.

God is in the bubbles. God is in me and my family, hidden deep but true, as we go about the business of the day.

A typical morning.

A Conversation

04 July 2019

I haven't seen you at the shelter recently."

"Yeah, well, I guess I don't see much point these days."

"Why not?"

"I don't think I believe it any more. To be honest, I don't really see how you can believe it."

"What do you mean? You've given up your faith?"

"There's a part of me, you know, that's always suspected that it was nonsense, and it just got harder and harder to ignore. Take the resurrection. That's ridiculous isn't it?"

"No."

"Come on. Even putting aside the ludicrous concept, you have to admit that it's hardly a convincing story. Luke says one thing, Mark says something else. They're all over the place."

"That's it? You're throwing it all in for that?"

"You make it sound like it's no big deal. Of course it's a big deal. What am I supposed to believe if the Bible can't even decide what it believes?"

"Look, you've got a shed, right?"

"A shed?"

"Yeah."

"Yes, I've got a shed. So what?"

"What do you keep in your shed?"

"What has this got to do-"

"Just bear with me. You'll see what I'm getting at."

"Fine. My lawnmower. Some tools. I don't know."

"Right, let's say someone broke into your shed and stole your lawnmower. Now let's say you talk to a bunch of people who were walking past your house at the time, and one says he saw someone in your garden around lunchtime, and someone else says no, no, no, it was well after lunch-"

"Stop right there. I've heard that all before, the tired old excuse about eyewitness accounts."

"That's not my point. My point is that it doesn't matter what the eyewitnesses say, you're still not able to mow your lawn, are you? That's the indisputable fact."

"That's probably the most ridiculous thing you've ever said."

"So. It's still true."

"But it's not enough."

"OK, well, why have you stopped coming to the shelter?"

"I told you. I don't believe it anymore."

"So you've stopped helping people? Sounds to me like not believing makes you a worse person."

"Are you seriously telling me that I should go on believing a lie because it makes me a better person?"

"No, I'm telling you that maybe the thing that makes you a worse person must be the lie."

The Ballad of the Handyman

11 July 2019

The workshop smelt of oil and sweat,

Of stone and wood and clay.

The tools of many disciplines,

Around, about they lay.

The handyman, he raised his head:

"How may I help today?"

"My plate," I said. "It fell. It broke.

Was nothing I could do."

I offered him the bag of shards,

Of red and green and blue:

"The task is beyond my skill, but

I hear good things of you."

The handyman, he took the bag,

He didn't say a word.

No words were needed if he was

As good as I had heard.

The twinkle in his eyes said an

Agreement had occurred.

Now the waiting brought misery;

All rain, and no rainbow.

How could I cope without my plate?

I didn't truly know.

For shards were better than nothing –

Why had I let it go?

Absence makes the heart grow fonder;

That's what they've always said,

And now that absent plate, it seemed,

To my fond heart was wed.

That handyman! If only I'd

Left something else instead!

But I consoled myself with hope

Of coming better days,

For my plate would soon be mended,

My heart repaired always.

If only the handyman would

Avoid needless delays!

The handyman! That handyman!

He'd sown a bitter crop!

But then the news, it came to me,

From that far-flung workshop.

The task had been completed and

My anguish – it could stop.

The workshop smelt of oil and sweat,

Of wood and clay and stone.

"My dear plate," I said. "Where is it?

I've come to take it home."

The handyman, he passed to me

The plate I had once known.

"What violence have you done to it?"

I screamed at what I saw,

For my soul, my beautiful plate,

Seemed beautiful no more.

The handyman was silent, like

One who'd been here before.

This was no plate! That villain! He'd

Made something else instead!

A fine mosaic formed of shards

Of green and blue and red.

"This isn't what I wanted, sir.

You've done me wrong!" I said.

The handyman, he frowned at this,

His voice boomed, dark and strong:

"You brought me shards, I gave my craft.

How have I done you wrong?

I'm the handyman. Why go back

Instead of going on?

"You say you heard good things of me?

You now think them untrue?

They're not. I think within your heart

You knew what I would do.

You see, my friend, I don't repair.

Behold! I make things new."

Now That's What James Calls Worship #1

18 July 2019

My friend Terry writes a blog and has been doing an enjoyable series of posts on Christian albums that have had an impact on him over the years. I've been thinking of doing something similar myself for a while, mostly as a follow-up to my own post about music from last year, but I didn't want to just copy Terry. That's not cool. So, instead I thought of something completely different and totally not related in any way to what Terry has been doing.

One of the things I've hinted at in the past is that there aren't many contemporary worship songs that I find helpful in drawing me into an attitude of praise. What I've decided to do is take a brief look at some individual songs that I have found particularly helpful (see – it's totally different to what Terry is doing).

First up is 'Lift' by *Mortal*.

I'm not really very good at defining bands by their genre or style, but Wikipedia tells me that *Mortal* is an 'industrial/dance band' which is probably as good as anything I could say. What I do know is that, musically, *Mortal* did an awful lot for me at a time when I was struggling to engage with the worship that I would typically find in church on a Sunday morning. Terry lists the album 'Fathom' as one of his favourites of all time, and I would agree with that. It's fantastic.

One of *Mortal*'s side projects was a band called *Jyradelix*, and 'Lift' appeared first (I believe) on that album in an early-90s rave edition. I prefer the crunchy intensity of the *Mortal* live version. Fair enough, it's not really built for congregational worship, but this is a style of music that speaks to me.

I'll admit that I'm not thrilled with the chorus:

God is love,

And love is God,

And He's invincible.

The 'And love is God' line is annoyingly ambiguous, but I know what I mean when I'm singing it, and so does God. However, I typically associate *Mortal* with lyrical artistry, and this song doesn't disappoint. For example:

Effecting and causing,

Almighty Lord of time and space,

Who was and is and is to come,

One Love worthy to be praised!

I feel like there's a tendency in modern contemporary worship to focus on praising God for what He has done for us. There's nothing wrong with that, of course, but these days I find myself getting more excited when we sing something that focuses on praising God for *who He is.* After all, even if God had done nothing for us, He'd still be worthy of praise. 'Lift' covers that base, and in spades, in the sections like the one above, which consist of nothing more than epithets. Honestly, 'Effecting and Causing'! What an absolute corker of a title to throw at God. I love it!

As I continue this series *Mortal* will probably pop up again, at least once more, so look out for that. In the meantime, if you want to know more about my musical tastes so that you can use that information against me, this is the series of blog posts to look out for.

Capturing Jesus

25 July 2019

Most attempts to put Jesus on film typically fail in one way or another, which is inevitable. If Jesus can't be contained by a tomb, then there's no way the screen can hold him. The gospels give us so many different aspects of Jesus' character, while filmmakers tend to fall into the trap of emphasising one or two aspects that mean the most to him or her. If the filmmaker wants to get across the fact that Jesus was a charismatic, joyful figure then the actor wanders across the Middle East with a goofy grin on his face *in every single scene*, while if a gracious, gentle Jesus is preferred then he is expected to make gooey eyes at every single person he meets. It's no wonder no-one has ever done the role justice.

Despite all this, most attempts to put the life of Christ on film have some redeemable features. I still have a soft spot for Franco Zeffirelli's 1977 epic *Jesus of Nazareth*, even though it gets a fair few things wrong. For example, it spends far too long on the birth narrative; it's so sllloooowwww that it's unwatchable, and even the star power of Darth Vader can't save it. There are also one or two questionable casting decisions, I think, and Robert Powell's portrayal of Jesus as a blue-eyed mystic is just creepy at times. However, on the plus side, there are a handful of moments that are so fantastic that every now and then the whole thing is lifted to sublime heights.

There's one compelling little scene in which Peter is getting ready for bed, muttering under his breath about an argument he's had with his wife, trying to convince himself that this Jesus thing is just something to do while the fishing is quiet. Matthew interrupts his rant to say something along the lines of, *"Peter, stop lying to yourself. Surely you've realised by now that none of us are going back to our old lives ever again. In fact, the whole world is never going to be same again."* It's not in the Bible, of course, but I love it anyway, because it's such a human moment, and at some point the disciples must have had this whole *'We're not in Kansas anymore'* conversation.

Another standout moment is the way that the series handles the telling the Parable of the Prodigal Son. It takes some dramatic license, as filmmakers do, by blending it with the calling of

Matthew (and putting Peter front and centre) but there's still so much that it gets right. I'm not a fan of James Farentino's attempt at Peter, but after watching this scene you can see exactly how parables had the power to melt hearts or drive people into a fury.

Speaking of fury, another great moment is when Robert Powell finally lets loose, after hours of drifting through Palestine like a stoned hippy, and accuses the scribes and Pharisees of hypocrisy. If you've ever struggled to understand exactly why the authorities wanted Jesus dead, watching a couple of minutes of *Jesus of Nazareth* will demonstrate it perfectly.

It's no surprise that each individual attempt to portray Jesus will only capture part of the picture. That's why God deals in communities, I suppose.

You are Contagious

01 August 2019

I'm going to take a blog break for a couple of weeks over the summer, starting after this post. This is the first break I've taken since I started in 2015, so I don't feel guilty at all. I'm going to leave you with a thought, something you can mull over while I'm off-line, and then we'll pick up with business as usual in a couple of weeks. OK? Good.

The thought is this: you are contagious.

Don't worry. So am I.

Have you ever met someone who seems only too keen to infect you with whatever mindset they're carrying? Someone who is, for example, particularly anxious about their life, and when you talk with them they begin to try and pass it on to you? I'm not talking about them trying to make you anxious about their life, but rather them trying to make you anxious about *your own life*. So you're telling them about what's going on for you, and they begin to tell you all the things that you should be worrying about. They want you to think about your own life in the way they think about theirs. It's like they have more anxiety in them than can be contained by one person, and it's itching to jump into your head.

The thing is, they can't help it. We all do it, without thinking most of the time. We're all contagious. Each of us meanders through life, bumping off one another like pebbles in a tumble dryer and what we carry in us rubs off on others.

So think about that. You are contagious; that's inescapable. What you can choose, however, is what you want to infect others *with*.

Anxiety or hope? Sorrow or joy? Conflict or peace?

It's up to you.

Now That's What James Calls Worship #2

22 August 2019

Thank you for your patience. Here's another little glimpse into my musical tastes.

'Dancing in Concert with the Infinite' by *DigHayZoose* - a track from the bizarrely-named album 'MagentaMantaLoveTree'. Now, there are twenty-two songs listed on the album, but many of them are just short samples ripped from various sources. This includes the first track, which is just a few seconds of music that sounds like it comes from an old vinyl LP or radio programme. So 'Dancing in Concert with the Infinite' is technically the first song on the album, despite being the second listed track. Are you with me so far? Good.

What's the relevance of this? Well, this ends up affirming something that I happen to believe – that if you're going to start something, start it with praise. I think that's a good habit, and it's nice to see *DigHayZoose* agreeing with me by putting the only overt worship song on the album right at the beginning.

So why do I like it? Again, it's a style of music that appeals to me. There's a kind of funk/grunge thing going on, and who doesn't love that opening bass/drum combo?

The lyrics wouldn't feel out of place in many churches these days, but there's something in this that I think is missing in much contemporary worship – there's a Trinitarian theology that flows naturally through the whole piece. It's just an assumed foundation. It doesn't feel forced or even intentional. It's just *there*. As with 'Lift', the previous entry in this series, it feels like some real thought about who God is went into this song.

I can even overlook the ridiculous fact that the song is listed as 'Dancing in Concert with the Infinate' on the back of the album. I think I probably care about spelling more than God does.

Feeling Emotional at the Airport

29 August 2019

I'm sitting in Gatwick airport in that limbo just before we're supposed to board our plane – that space when you're simultaneously on holiday and not on holiday. It's Schrodinger's Holiday. As I sit here, I'm reading Jesus' words in John 12:24-28.

"The man who loves his life will lose it, while the man who hates his life in this world will keep it for eternal life."

As I read those words I am overwhelmed with a sense of longing for the next world. It feels like homesickness.

I look up, and I see a dad walking along, suitcase in tow, with his young daughter following close behind. She's dressed in the kind of clothes that only a child can get away with wearing, including some outrageous hat with giant eyes on it. I think it's supposed to be a Disney character or something.

I'm in a vulnerable state. I think about my own daughters, and realise that while they are still in the Disney age bracket, it won't last forever. They will soon be grown-up and no longer able to get away with dressing like a cartoon animal. They will soon be grown-up and no longer trotting loyally after dad. This realisation makes me sad.

Strange place, Gatwick. I'm feeling homesick for a place I've never seen, and a sense of loss over something that I still have.

I blame the early start.

Partying Out In the Open

05 September 2019

There's a line in Nehemiah 12, when the people of Judah are celebrating the dedication of Jerusalem's wall, that reads like this: "The sound of rejoicing in Jerusalem could be heard far away."

In the Old Testament, in verses like Exodus 19:6 and Deuteronomy 4:5-8, it's clear that what God intends for His people is for them to be a community that draws other nations to Himself. I think that's always God's agenda – drawing people to Himself. Sometimes, like the nation of Israel, his contemporary followers think that God's purpose is for them to withdraw into a sanctified huddle, to dispense judgement and moral instruction on the world from afar. It's almost as if some of us think that Jesus stood up in Nazareth and declared:

"The Spirit of the LORD is upon me,

because He has anointed me

to put up walls between myself and the rest of society."

Well, he didn't.

I'm not renowned for drawing people into the community of God, and I am certainly prone to letting things get on top of me, but I am also convinced that I have plenty to rejoice about, and if there's one thing that gets people's attention, it's a party – particularly in days when it seems like there's not much to celebrate.

John Bunyan said, "I have often thought that the best Christians are found in the worst of times" and I think he was right. During difficult days, a follower of Jesus will find something to rejoice about, and the sound of a party carries a long way on the wind.

Then God gets to turn to the rest of the world and say, "Do you like what you hear? Well, come and join my party."

Now That's What James Calls Worship #3

12 September 2019

The album version of this track isn't available on YouTube (not in the UK, at least) so I'm having to post a live version taken from a festival, which is somewhat at odds with what the song means for me, as I'll go on to explain.

Anyway, the band is *Selfmindead* and the song is called 'Always'.

The advantage with worship that is centred around who God is and what He's done is that it's always suitable for congregational singing. It doesn't matter how I'm feeling, what is true about God remains true. Sometimes, however, I need worship that is a bit more situational, a bit more personal. Sometimes I like to withdraw and spend some time thinking about what's going on between me and God, right here and right now, in a private setting, and express that through worship.

This song, 'Always', is one of my go-to songs when I'm wanting to let God know that, when it comes down to it, all I really want is to be in His presence. This song is about how just being with God is enough to shift my perspective and calm my fears. It's strange to see this song being performed live, complete with crowd-surfers and audience participation, because for me this track is about a very personal experience.

It's built on a metaphor of being in a garden with God. The line '*Your garden is beautiful. All I want is to be here with You*' is one that my soul can't help but say 'Amen' to every time I hear it.

If you've listened to the track then you may feel that the gentle, pastoral lyrics are incongruous with the aggressive, heavy style of music. I do like this style, but it's also worth noting that music that sounds angry isn't always being angry. In this case, it's almost as if the music provides a cathartic way of getting through the chaos and confusion of life to the soul-affirming peace and calm that comes from finding yourself in the presence of the Living God. This is heavy music that gives me a light heart.

If you can't make out the lyrics (I understand if you can't…) then you can find them on-line. They lack the theological sophistication of my previous picks, but in terms of putting words into my mouth about just how much I need to be with God, and how desperate I am to be in His presence, they more than do the job.

Your face gives me comfort,

Your arms give me rest,

Your word is my foundation,

Your name is alive.

Yes, everyone should have a song that helps them just *be* with God.

Do I Want to Preach?

19 September 2019

Now that's a tricky question.

The thing is, I'm not sure that I do. Sometimes, over the years, people have asked me if I enjoy preaching. 'Enjoy' is not the word I would use.

There's always a level of satisfaction that comes from doing something that you can actually do. I've spent fair chunks of my working life on things that I'm not actually very good at, but I *can* preach. It's nice to be allowed to be competent every once in a while.

But there's more to it than that. I feel very strongly that preaching is not just something I *can* do, it's something that I *should* be doing. I don't really ever know that I would say it was a 'calling', because to me that implies some sort of exclusivity; that my preaching is my primary expression of my faith – the most important thing that I do. That's not true. The most important thing that I do, and my true 'calling', is to try and live a life of obedience to Jesus in every single second of every single day. Preaching is just a part of that.

But I genuinely think that God wants me to preach.

So it's something of a problem that He doesn't seem to care whether *I* want to do it or not.

Tricky.

If I were to sit down after a sermon one day, and God were to say to me, "You know what, James, you don't ever have to do that again." I would be quite relieved and very pleased. If it were up to me, I would probably never say anything in public, ever.

But at the moment, if I were to stop preaching there would be something hollow about me, like a pencil that's missing its lead, and that scares me more than the thought of having to stand up and bear the responsibility of opening my mouth.

Do I enjoy preaching? Do I want to preach? No, not really, but I *have* to do it. That's about all I can say: I *have* to do it. Not for the first time in my life, I feel like that when I get to heaven, I'll be spending a bit of time comparing notes with Jeremiah…

But if I say, "I will not mention him

or speak any more in his name,"

his word is like a fire in my bones.

I am weary of holding it in;

indeed, I cannot.

Jeremiah 20:9

Sometimes the Niceness if the Point...

26 September 2019

Today I am repenting of my bad memory. I had allowed myself to forget something important.

I had not forgotten that God is kind, or that He is generous, or that He loves me. No, it was something else.

I had forgotten that sometimes God does nice things just to do nice things.

I was beginning to allow a false god to creep into my life. A god who was kind and generous and loving, but false because he was also eminently and irredeemably sensible. The false god was my favourite uncle, who never forgot my birthday and was always generous with his gifts, but...but when I sat down to open the present it was clothes, or a science kit, or a subscription to an educational magazine. This god never gave anything frivolous or fun for fun's sake. This was the false god I had been allowing to move into my life. The god who smiled patiently at me and said, "I'm glad you're having fun, James, but shouldn't we get on with something a bit more constructive now…"

I had forgotten, you see, a particular thing that happened to me once. A time when God gave me something specific in response to a prayer that He invited me to pray. Something kind and something generous, but ultimately something utterly pointless. My life was not meaningfully enriched by it. The possession of this thing did not make me more like Christ. There was no secret purpose or divine providence behind it, other than to show me that sometimes God is just nice.

And recently, when I was allowing myself to worship this false god, the god who always had my best intentions at heart, and therefore became concerned when it looked like I was enjoying myself a little too much, the real God showed up. He reminded me who He was, and that sometimes He did nice, but totally unnecessary, things.

I had forgotten, you see, that He is not just the God who looks out of the window in the morning and says, "Are you going outside today? You'd better take a jumper because it looks a bit chilly." He is also the God of water fights, and jokes that go nowhere, and lazy afternoons spent lying on the sofa watching TV.

Sometimes God gives for the sake of seeing a smile on our faces, and the smile is the only point.

I had forgotten that, and I repent.

Now That's What James Calls Worship #4

03 October 2019

I hope you're in the mood for some electropop. This one is by *Joy Electric* and is called 'I'm Your Boy'.

This is like the previous entry ('Always') but even more so, in that this is not one that would even begin to work with a congregation. For starters, the title alone rules out 50% of the population being able to sing it as written.

Unlike the first three entries in this series, there's nothing in this that can be considered 'praise' as such. It's purely a declaration of commitment to God, and a fairly courageous one if you take the words seriously (*When all else denies You, I'm Your boy. When the world declines You, I'm Your boy*). For me, offering this pledge to God is as much an act of worship as anything else.

One of the reasons I like the Psalms is their ability to put into words the deepest stirrings of my soul when I myself am tongue-tied. It's great to be able to borrow someone else's creativity and think

"That's exactly how I feel…" Just as 'Always' gives voice to my desire to be with God, so 'I'm Your Boy' gives voice to my genuine longing to be faithful and committed to Him, despite the cost.

Being truly bonded to God is not an easy or straightforward thing. Saying 'Yes' to God means saying 'No' to the alternatives that the world offers, and that'll come back to bite you in many unexpected and unusual ways over the years. However, *Joy Electric* has you covered:

Have a friend who never ends,

The love He once for all began,

So jump for joy,

The party's for the poor boys.

That idea (*The party's for the poor boys*) comes straight out of the Beatitudes, and for those of us who want to follow Jesus, that's a good place to look for hope when the world pushes back.

Without Words

10 October 2019

For someone who likes words, I seem to spend a lot of my time not able to find the right ones.

Many of my days are spent searching for perfect words, and then trying to arrange them in the perfect order. There are plenty of moments where I can't even seem to find adequate words, let alone perfect ones. Ask anyone who's spent part of their life trying to have a conversation with me and they'll tell that you that patience is a prerequisite. I'm very conscious of the frequency with which I make people wait in silence while I rack my brains for the combination of words that is *just right*.

God gets it worse than anyone else. He has to deal with me when I am overwhelmed by a swirling maelstrom of emotion and thought, and struggling to put it all into prayer. Paul tells the Romans that when we don't know what to pray, the Spirit intercedes for us with wordless groans. Maybe, but a lot of the time I can't even manage to find the right groan.

In Canterbury Cathedral there's a stained glass window that captures a moment from the life of

Jesus. He's at a table, and crouched at his feet is a woman, and those of us familiar with the story know that she's weeping, bathing his feet with her tears and drying them with her hair.

There are no words in that cathedral window. There are no words in that story, at least not from the woman. There are words from Jesus and words from the guests at the meal who are outraged by her behaviour, but there are no words from her. Words are unnecessary. Her tears are her prayer; each drop a blend of unspoken syllables and meaning; each splash heard and perfectly understood by the Son of God.

That thought is of immense comfort to me every time I sit in front of that window, without words, and try to make sense of what's going on inside me. The confusion that I can't unravel is my prayer to God, and it already makes perfect sense to Him.

The Little Things

17 October 2019

Clickity clickity clickity click. Michael's hands rolled across the keyboard like an express train. On the screen in front of him the numbers spontaneously appeared in the grid. Cause and effect. Michael remembered a time, in his university days, where he had got into an argument about the beauty of numbers. The purest form of poetry, he had said. The numbers never lie, he had said. They always mean what they say and say what they mean, he had said. He may have then made a derogatory comment about a girl he used to go out with. He couldn't quite remember. It was a long time ago, and he had been a bit drunk.

Yes, a long time ago. These days he didn't feel quite the same way about numbers. Years and years in front of a computer, making the digits dance before his very eyes, had taken some of the shine off. Nothing kills passion like turning a hobby into a living. The numbers he worked with now certainly told stories, but they only told the whole truth and nothing but the truth, and when you want an exciting story a little lie every now and then makes all the difference in the world.

He looked up, to the window behind the computer screen. It was still raining on the grey street of houses. Not much of a view, if it were not for the bus shelter right in the centre of his field of vision. Bus stops told stories too, and they could be quite exciting, though you never knew the honesty of them. The bus shelter was there for when the numbers became just that bit too boring.

No people waiting for buses now; no-one sitting in the shelter. He glanced at the clock. The 11:17 must have passed by without him realising. At least fifteen minutes until the next one. No stories for the moment, just the rain dancing. With some interest he noted that a pool of water had gathered at the side of the shelter's right-hand support, a marriage of the rain and the overflow from the shelter's roof. A happy marriage this one, he figured.

Entering the window from Michael's left came a small, snugly-wrapped figure in wellington boots. Michael took immediate notice. A child, maybe three or four years old? At that age the rain was a source of joy rather than damp feet and misery. The tiny actor moved quickly, centre stage, hand brushing playfully against the bus stop and shelter, and halted at the edge of the newly formed lake. Anticipation swelled in Michael. There was only one outcome for this scenario. This small adventurer knew what to do when confronted with a puddle.

The tiny figure studied the water with all the interest of a professional. The numbers forgotten, Michael felt himself drift forward, to the literal edge of his seat.

Then, just as the tension had become unbearable, it happened – a leap that took the combined effort of all the growing muscles in this small thing, and a sudden downward stamp right into the middle of the puddle. Then again! Jump! Splash! Again! Jump! Splash! Again, again, again! Michael imagined he could see, deep in the hooded periscope of the child's coat, twinkling eyes and a smile. Was it a boy child or a girl child? Michael couldn't tell, and – frankly – he didn't care. When it came to joy, the rain was an equal opportunities employer. As Michael watched this enthusiastic moment, a warm glow and a gormless smile engulfed him.

Then, Entering Stage Left, approached a banshee. She stormed (there was no other word) to the bus shelter and grabbed the child by the elbow. Even through the rain, from the other side of the road, Michael could hear the shrill declaration:

"Come on! We don't have time for this! We have to get your brother!"

Then the banshee Exited Stage Right dragging the small bundle by the arm, the wellington boots engaged in a mad quickstep to keep up with angry mum.

Michael stared at the rain, the bus shelter and the puddle long after its waters had calmed. He stared until there was a lump in his throat and his eyes glazed over. Then, swallowing hard, he went back to the numbers.

A Letter to My Struggling Sister or Brother

24 October 2019

ear Sister/Brother,

There is something that I want to say to you.

When I decided to follow Jesus as an awkward teenager (really, is there any other kind of teenager?) I had only one redeeming quality. It wasn't that I was quite clever, or reasonably likeable, or that I had a glistening ball of potential creativity resting in me. None of those things have ultimately been of much consequence. The one and only ace I think I've ever had (and I suspect the primary reason why I'm still here writing stuff like this after some rather brutal periods of having everything conspire to make following Jesus an extremely unattractive option) is that when I threw my lot in with the rejected messiah, I pretty much said, "I'm in, and if I'm in then I really mean it, and if I'm in then I really want it."

It may not seem like much when you weigh it up, but I'm convinced that it's been the difference maker for most of my life. What has kept me going over the years, even when I have failed to live up to my own expectations, has not been any gifting or great learning, but a yearning for the vast and endless ocean; a small but significant, deep, unceasing, burning desire to see God. I've learnt a lot of theology over the years, some of it quite useful, but I suspect none of it has been as useful as the sheer bloody-mindedness to keep going and going and going until God and His promises prove to be real. You see, knowledge is very good and to be treasured, but when you hit a roadblock in your spiritual life, it's often only the man or woman armed with a genuine desire for God who will find a way through.

In all the bruising experiences of existence, what has kept me moving forward has not been some delusion or clever piece of psychological trickery, rather it's been a sort of spiritual stubbornness; the part of me that really meant it when I said I was in. I've felt like giving up on almost everything I've ever done at some point, but not God. Sometimes I've clung on by my fingernails, but I've clung on to Him with the same conviction by which He has clung on to me. Only once in my life have I pulled the stroppy teenager act on God, and even then I couldn't do it properly.

You see, I've always trusted (and when I haven't trusted, I've suspected) that God would come through somehow someday. When I have been stuck halfway up the mountain, exhausted and surrounded by darkness, unable to see where to put my foot next, I've known that if I can keep going then, one day, I would get through that cloud cover and reach the peak and see that glorious starlit night sky, and that's proven to be the case more times than I can count. That's what has kept me coming back to God even when sanity has seemed to demand otherwise.

It's just a hunger and a thirst for Jesus. That's all. Not doctrine or expectation or learned behaviour and churchy culturisation, but simple hunger and thirst. I've built many boats, and set out on the ocean many times, and every time I've been dumped into the cold, salty water and found myself spluttering on the shore again, my reaction has been to get up and build another boat, not because I love boats, but because I just have to be on the ocean. I can't live on dry land any more. I haven't been able to for years now.

What I've wanted to say to you is this:

If you find yourself lying awake at night, restlessly dissatisfied with where you're at at the moment…if you have nothing more than a twisting, squirming desire for God in you that makes you so uncomfortable that you sometimes wonder how you can sleep at night…if you want nothing more than to lay hold of a Jesus who seems so far away right now…you know who you are, and what I want to say to you is that there are far worse places to be. Take heart. I think you'll be alright. Blessed are those who hunger and thirst for righteousness, for they <u>will</u> be filled.

Your foolish but stubborn brother,

James

About the Author

James is a writer, a father, a husband, a follower of Jesus and a lover of board games, though not necessarily in that order. Sometimes he even manages to do some of these things quite well. He's crammed quite a lot of experiences into his life so far, such as working for Tearfund; being a Baptist minister; living in Australia as part of a mission and discipleship community and watching Q.P.R. beat Oldham Athletic at Loftus Road on the 27th December 1993. It's not been all bad.

He and his family currently live in Canterbury, England.

JAMES WEBB

Books by the Same Author

The Listening Book:
The Soul Painting & Other Stories

This is a beautiful book, in words and images, and will appeal to old and young and all those in between. As the title suggests, the stories are perfect for reading aloud and could be used in a range of settings. The delicate images add another dimension. From fables to folk tales, from stories told around the camp fire to John Lewis Christmas ads, humankind responds to the power of story and to the meaning that narratives give us.

Sophie Duffy
Author of *Bright Stars*, *The Generation Game* and *This Holey Life*.

Job 28 pictures the search for wisdom as digging for gold. The Listening Book has numerous nuggets to mine, embedded in stories that will help you to remember them.

Steve Divall
Senior Pastor, St Helen's Church, North Kensington.

Hardback ISBN: 978-0-9934383-0-1   Softback ISBN: 978-0-9934383-2-5
EBook ISBN: 978-0-9934383-1-8 Audiobook via Amazon/Audible
Religion: Inspirational
Lioness Writing Ltd Release date: 31 October 2015
144 pages, 8.5 inches x 8.5 inches, 25 colour photographs and 3 B&W photos

The Second Listening Book: Loaded Question & Other Stories

I enjoy reading James Webb, not just because he is a gifted and imaginative storyteller, but because he provides nourishing soul food for the journeys we all make through the deserts of life. With his creative imagination he provokes a range of emotions in the reader and I invite you to step inside and be prepared to find something for which your soul has cried out.

David Coffey OBE
Global Ambassador for BMS World Mission.

There are very few books I read that can make me laugh and think profoundly at the same time. This book however is one of them. As a child I used to watch Tales of the Unexpected and loved the twists at the end - James' book easily surpasses them. It is very easy to read and yet worthwhile at the same time as each story contains spiritual truths (which aren't at all preachy and sometimes not obvious!). This is a book you have to try - you won't regret it.

Eric Harmer
Pastor of Barton Church, Canterbury and Author of
Build-Your-Own Bible Study.

Hardback ISBN: 978-0-9934383-6-3   Softback ISBN: 978-0-9934383-4-9
EBook ISBN: 978-0-9934383-7-0 Audiobook via Amazon/Audible
Religion: Inspirational
Lioness Writing Ltd Release date: 31 October 2016
158 pages, 8.5 inches x 8.5 inches, 31 black & white illustrations and photos

The Ramblings of the Man who Bought a Pear

James's Blog started in October 2015 and became a weekly phenomenon that adds salt and light to the internet. This first year of posts is a rich collection of things in his head that he was brave enough to release into the wild. 'The Man who Sold me a Pear' won the 2016 Association of Christian Writers 'Good Samaritan' short story award in partnership with Street Pastors.

www.thelisteningbook.org.uk

The Association of Christian Writers is a fellowship of writers sharing prayerful support and encouragement as well as giving professional standards of training and advice. They support Christian writers overseas, in the developing world and Eastern Europe. www.christianwriters.org.uk

Street Pastors are trained volunteers from local churches who serve their community during the small hours of the weekend. Teams of men and women patrol from 10 pm to 4 am on a Friday and Saturday night, to care for, listen to and help people who are out on the streets. Proceeds from this book will help support this work. www.streetpastors.org

Comments on 'The Man who Sold me a Pear':
Anne: I had a tear in my eye too!
Jon: Can really relate to this one. Thanks for writing it.
David: I just discovered your Blog. Love it and the honesty in sharing your life and faith. This story about buying a pear really touched me. Cheers James.

Softback £5.99/$10 ISBN: 978-0-9934383-8-7
Religion: Inspirational
Published by Lioness Writing Ltd, Member of CSPA
<lionesswritingltd@gmail.com>
Release date: 31 October 2016
170 pages
8 inches x 5 inches

The Ramblings of the Man who Likes to Eat Alone

James's Blog then carried on for a second year. So that is what is in this book.

Softback £5.99/$10 ISBN: 978-1-9997464-1-4
Religion: Inspirational
Published by Lioness Writing Ltd,
Member of CSPA <lionesswritingltd@gmail.com>
Release date: 30 November 2017
148 pages
8 inches x 5 inches

The Ramblings of the Man who Isn't Very Good at Making Beds

…and then for a third year – the charm.

Softback £5.99/$10 ISBN: 978-1-9997464-4-5
Religion: Inspirational
Published by Lioness Writing Ltd,
Member of CSPA <lionesswritingltd@gmail.com>
Release date: 30 November 2018
174 pages
8 inches x 5 inches

More Posts

www.thelisteningbook.org.uk

You can contact James at

author@thelisteningbook.org.uk